Instant Expert

PHOTO SKILLS

Beatrice Haverich

A & C BLACK

Published by:
A & C Black
Bloomsbury Publishing Plc
49–51 Bedford Square
London WC1B 3DP

www.acblack.com

First published 2011

Original concept: Paul Mason
Project management: Paul Mason
Design: Mayer Media

ISBN   HB 9781408147207
        PB 9781408147191

A CIP record for this book is available from the
British Library.

This book is produced using paper made from
wood grown in managed, sustainable forests.
It is natural, renewable, and recyclable. The
logging and manufacturing processes conform
to the environmental regulations of the
country of origin.

Printed and bound in Malaysia by
Tien Wah Press

Photo acknowledgements:
All photos © Beatrice Haverich, except cover
photos Shutterstock; page 24 © Louis Kerr;
page 30 © Vanessa Jones.

Contents

Why become a
photography expert?

Ever wondered why what you see with your eyes does not look the same in your photographs? Or taken a nice portrait photo of your friend, only to find the background is so cluttered that it distracts from his or her face? If you're a happy snapper but want to create stronger images, then read on and master the art of photography.

FYI!
These features are scattered throughout the book. They contain information you can casually drop into conversation to amaze, astound, and impress your friends.

IMPRESS YOUR FRIENDS BY HELPING THEM

Whether you use a camera phone, a digital compact camera or a digital SLR, you will find out how to use the rules of photography to create stronger images. This book can teach you how to capture movement and interesting viewpoints, and how to recognize the perfect light for your landscape and portrait photography. Not only that, you'll also be able to give your friends photography tips, too!

Almost anything can be turned into a great subject for a photo, using the tricks and tips contained in this book.

SAVE CASH AND TIME

Digital cameras have lowered the cost of photography. Now, if you take a bad photo, you can bin it or work on it on a computer to improve it. However, by learning about framing and other technical tricks, more of your photos will turn out well. You will also save time spent sitting in front of a computer using photo-editing software.

FINDING THE RIGHT INFO

At the back of the book there is a **Troubleshooting** section. Maybe your photos are coming out with mistakes, such as being under- or overexposed, or with movement blurred? **Troubleshooting** tells you where to look for a fix. Or, if you know where the problem lies (camera functions, subject matter etc.), just use the contents page or index to go straight to the relevant place.

ALL KINDS OF CAMERA

Whatever kind of digital camera you use, you will find this book crammed with interesting information. Advice on choosing the right camera setting, deciding on the best viewpoint and angle, technical tips for SLR camera owners and sneaky insider '**Secret Tricks**' will keep your photography well above the rest. So go on – pick up your camera and get ready to become an instant expert.

 WATCH AN EXPERT!
Throughout the book these panels point you towards web pages where you can see the relevant skills being put into practice.

TOOLS FOR THE JOB
Sometimes, special equipment or camera settings will make your photography better or easier. These are listed in panels like this one.

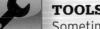 **LOST FOR WORDS**
look here for explanations of those tricky, technical words

Types of cameras

You might be using a phone camera that only works on automatic, or a compact camera with a variety of settings. Or you might be using a more advanced digital SLR camera. These give the photographer control over how the camera works, so you can pick the right settings to take the perfect photo.

Crucial tools for photography include:
- A camera
- Camera case to protect your camera
- Memory card for storing images

BE CREATIVE WITH YOUR PHONE

Camera phones are very simple to use. The camera settings are automatic (though some phone cameras do have the option of zooming in or using flash to brighten a dark scene). This lets you concentrate on composing the photo, trying out different viewpoints and finding interesting angles.

MORE OPTIONS ON A DIGITAL COMPACT

You can set a compact camera to automatic, in the same way as a camera phone. However, compact cameras also give you the choice to pick programme settings such as portrait if you have decided to take close-ups of faces. They usually also have settings for landscape, macro (close-up), sports and night scenery.

exposure how much light a camera lens lets in
shutter speed how quickly a camera lens works
SLR short for Single Lens Reflex

SECRET TRICK

When choosing a camera, look out for a good lens. This will make a real difference to your photography. However many features the camera has, you will not be able to take sharp, good-quality images if it does not have a good lens.

TECHNICAL TRICKERY WITH A DIGITAL SLR

Digital SLRs have the same settings as a compact camera, plus further controls. Expert photographers can control the amount of light the camera lets in (called the **exposure**), the speed at which the camera takes the photo (**shutter speed**), or both. This gives the photographer total control of how the image looks. On an SLR you can also change the camera's lens, giving you even more control over how the image comes out.

1 If you are buying a SLR camera, spend less on the camera body and invest in a good lens instead.

2 With compact cameras, choose the camera for its lens.

Find out which lenses are best by speaking to experts at your local camera shop. Once you have a shortlist of two or three cameras, visit Internet review sites to see what expert reviewers think of your choices.

FYI!
The smallest digital camera is shorter and narrower than a credit card – but it is a bit thicker!

The **story** of **photography**

Photography has been around for less than 200 years. Since it first began to appear in the early 1800s, photography has developed rapidly. Recently, the development of digital cameras has opened up photography to a vast new audience.

THE FIRST PHOTOGRAPHS

In 1826 French inventor Joseph Nicéphore Niépce used a **camera obscura** to take the first photograph. Then in early 1839 Louis-Jacques-Mandé Daguerre photographed a Paris street scene from his apartment window, using his newly invented 'daguerreotype' process. The long exposure time of several minutes meant moving objects didn't appear in the photo – but a man having a shoeshine stayed still long enough to become the first person ever photographed.

'The Horse in Motion' by Eadweard Muybridge was the first set of photos to show movement, in 1878.

THE FIRST COLOUR AND MOTION PHOTOGRAPHS

In 1861, the Scottish physicist James Clerk Maxwell created the first colour photograph by superimposing three black-and-white images, then passing them through red, green and blue filters. (Today, most electronic images are recorded in red-green-blue, or RGB.) Seventeen years later, Eadweard Muybridge set up 12 cameras to capture the movement of a running horse. A trip wire triggered each camera's shutter as the horse passed by.

📄 **camera obscura**
lightproof box with a small hole that lets through enough light to make an upsidedown image

A Kodak 'Box Brownie' camera.

SECRET HISTORY

These are some of the key dates in the development of photography during the 1900s.

• **1962**: *National Geographic* magazine publishes its first all-colour edition.

• **1963**: Polaroid produces the instant camera and colour film.

• **1991**: After years of photographing on film, photography finally hits the digital age. Kodak brings out the first digital camera for the professional market.

• **1994**: The first digital cameras become available for non-professional photographers.

HAND-HELD CAMERAS

In 1889 George Eastman, founder of the film and camera company Kodak, invented a flexible, unbreakable roll of film. The film allowed several images to be taken and stored inside a camera. Kodak then developed the 'Brownie' camera, often called the Box Brownie because of its boxy shape. The Brownie was very popular, and various models remained on sale until the 1960s. It was the Brownie that started the interest in photography among ordinary people that continues today.

FYI!
The first-ever photograph, taken in 1826, took eight hours to make!

George Eastman, founder of the photography company Kodak.

Pick a **point of interest**

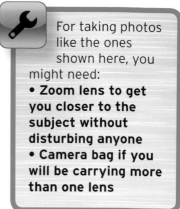

For taking photos like the ones shown here, you might need:
• **Zoom lens to get you closer to the subject without disturbing anyone**
• **Camera bag if you will be carrying more than one lens**

Always try to make sure your photographs give a clear message. For example, at a dog show you might want a photo of the winning dog. You would get as close as possible to the dog (or zoom in), to make the dog central to the image. You would also try to include something to show that he or she is the winner, such as a rosette.

SATURDAY MORNING MARKET PHOTOS
These images are all taken at a Saturday morning market, which is a great place for a photographer to practise finding a point of interest for his or her images. Some have a clearer focus than others.

MESSAGE LOST
This scene shows a dog waiting for its owner, but the dog is not the main focus. Choosing a different angle, zooming in, or crouching down would have emphasised the dog and its point of view.

MESSAGE CLEAR
Be brave, go inside the shop, compliment the staff on their produce, and ask if it's okay to take pictures.

ZOOM IN
Use your zoom lens to get closer to people. Capturing action, like this lady putting apples in her bag, makes a photo more engaging.

CHANGE YOUR POINT OF VIEW

Remember to crouch down at times for a different point of view. Here the focus is on the displayed books, but the photo also captures the seller and the relaxed atmosphere of a Saturday street market.

SPOT ODD ITEMS GROUPED TOGETHER

This is a real junk-stall display. Tennis balls, a fan, china, and an old slide projector are all grouped on one table. They make an excellent still-life photo.

SECRET TRICK

Looking at advertising photography is a good way to study how professional photographers make sure their photographs have a clear subject.

1 Advertising photos have to show the main product or the message of an advertising campaign as clearly as possible.

2 The photo above portrays the current youth culture. The emphasis is on the game console and head set, in the centre of the frame. The colourful baseball cap adds a different texture and brings the image to life.

CAPTURE INTERACTION

This photograph shows not only the display of bread, but also both the buyer and seller.

Keep it **simple**

Make sure that only the things you want the viewer to see appear in your photos. If there are lots of objects cluttering up the background, your message will be lost. This is particularly true of portrait shots, where you do not want anything distracting from your main subject.

For making your subject stand out against a blurry background, you can use:
- **Telephoto/zoom lens**
- **Camera's 'portrait' setting**

CAMERA ANGLE
Consider changing your camera angle to compose your picture with a non-distracting background, or choose a more suitable background:

In this shot, the viewer's eyes are drawn to the chimney behind the head of the boy.

By stepping to the side and slightly changing the camera angle, this photographer has given the image a less distracting background.

DEPTH OF FIELD
Using an SLR camera's settings you can give photos a shallow **depth of field**. This de-clutters the background by making it blurry. There are three ways to do this.
1) Aperture: more open apertures = shallower depth of field. An open aperture between f/2.8 and f/4 will give a blurry background.
2) Choice of lens: longer lenses, such as telephoto/zoomed-in lenses, have a small zone of sharpness and blur backgrounds well.
3) Distance to the subject: an object near the camera, with the background a long way behind, will appear sharp with a blurry background.

aperture mechanism inside the lens controlling amount of light coming in
depth of field distance between the nearest and farthest objects that are in sharp focus

To find out more about using depth of field to enhance your photos, check out: **www.acblack.com/instantexpert**

VARYING DEPTH OF FIELD

1) The focus is on the object in front of the lens, with an open aperture of f/5.6 and a 50mm lens, standing as close as possible. The background appears slightly blurred.

2) The focus is again on the plant in front of the lens. A more open aperture of f/4, combined with an 85mm lens, minimizes what is in focus and throws the background out of focus.

3) The focus is still in front of the lens, but with a small aperture of f/14, a 24mm lens and the photographer standing further back from the main subject, far more of the background is in focus.

SECRET TRICK

It is possible to use a compact camera's setting to take photos with a blurred background. Just choose the portrait symbol, which automatically produces an open aperture. Next, zoom in as much as you can and stand as close as possible to your subject.

1 Here, the subject and the background compete for the viewer's attention. The tree and fence distract from the portrait.

2 With the camera in portrait mode, and the image zoomed in, the background is thrown into soft focus and is less distracting.

Consider **contrast**

To add contrast to digital photos you could use:
- **Exposure-compensation button on SLR camera**
- **Photo-editing software**

Contrasts of all kinds can give your photos more impact. Dark subjects look stronger placed in front of a light background and vice versa. Contrasting colours can have the same effect (though make sure they're not distracting). Even contrasting the photo subject and context – an old granny on a roller coaster, for example – can enhance your photography. Here are some examples.

LIGHT AND SHADOW
The contrast between light and shadow makes this picture of a road far more interesting. The photo shows well-balanced contrast, including whites and blacks.

CONTRASTING COLOURS
In both of these images, the bright colours complement each other and create the feeling of fun, summer and holidays.

LIGHT AGAINST DARK
The sunlit, icy trees stand out in front of the dark, unlit woods behind. Here the contrast is provided by a combination of the subject and the lighting difference between **high key** at the front of the image and **low key** at the back.

high key mostly light, including white
low key mostly dark, including black

LIGHT ON LIGHT

This photograph of a snow-covered bench does not work well because it does not have enough contrast. The bench disappears into the snowy background, as the light is very dull. A touch of sunlight on the back of the bench would have increased the contrast and made a better photo.

SECRET TRICK

You can alter contrast using Photoshop, or other image-editing software, after you have taken the photograph. Here's how to do it in Photoshop:

1 Open up your image in Photoshop. Go to the *Image* menu, scroll down to *Adjustments*, open up *Brightness and Contrast*, and either increase or decrease your contrast as needed.

After increasing the contrast using Photoshop, the light and dark areas are more defined, and the snow is cleaner looking than in the version on the left.

DARK ON DARK

Here, the black night sky makes the bright colours stand out and creates an atmospheric photograph. Try out your compact camera's 'night' setting to get results like this.

2 Be careful not to overdo contrast. Push it too far and you will get burnt-out areas (parts of the image where no detail is visible).

Ansel Adams
photography

Most photographers like to take pictures of nature. How about giving your pictures real meaning? The American environmentalist and photographer Ansel Adams expressed his love for nature using his camera. Known as the 'Master of Photography', Adams's technical skill was legendary. However, it is the powerful message of his photographs that makes his work so inspiring.

Yosemite Falls.

'Simply look with perceptive eyes at the world about you, and trust to your own reactions and convictions. Ask yourself: "Does this subject move me to feel, think and dream?"'
Ansel Adams

ADAMS AND YOSEMITE

Adams got his first camera, a Kodak No.1 Box Brownie, from his parents. A keen hiker, climber and explorer, Adams used the camera when he visited Yosemite Valley, California, in 1916. Yosemite, a beautiful wilderness in northern California, was then little known to the American public. His interest in Yosemite led Adams to become friends with many of the founders of America's conservation movement, and he was soon involved in their campaigns to preserve America's wild places.

**Yosemite Valley,
Yosemite National Park.**

PHOTOGRAPHY AND THE ENVIRONMENT

Adams photographed mostly in black and white. His photographic style echoed nineteenth-century American landscape painting and photography. He used his images to stimulate interest in America's environmental issues, National Parks and the preservation of wildernesses. Adams fought for new National Parks, the Wilderness Act, Wild Alaska, and the preservation of redwood forests, as well as for endangered species like sea lions.

ADAMS'S LEGACY

Adams's enthusiasm for saving the magnificent beauty of the American West, and his hope that humans could live in harmony with the environment, struck a chord with the American people. Today Adams is still respected as a visual artist and conservationist.

**Manley Beacon from
Zabriskie Point, Death
Valley National Park.**

What is **framing?**

A 'frame' in a photograph is something in the foreground that leads you into the picture or gives you a sense of where the viewer is. A tree branch with leaves framing a shot of rolling hills or a valley, a river leading into a landscape, or houses on the side of a street in an urban setting can all be used to frame a photo.

! If you remember one thing about framing images, make it:
- **Frames work well when they are out of focus**

FRAMING IN AN INDUSTRIAL SETTING
The boats are leading the viewer's eyes to the chimney. This photo was taken with a compact camera on a landscape setting.

FRAMING AN IMAGE
When framing a photo, make sure you focus on the subject rather than the frame! To do this, focus on the subject, then hold your **shutter button** halfway down to keep the focus the same. Next, compose your picture before pushing the button fully down and taking the photo.

≡ **shutter button** trigger for the shutter mechanism of the camera

FRAMING IN A RURAL SETTING
Here the diagonal fence leads the viewer's eye into a rural landscape, towards the horizon.

CONSIDER FRAMING IN A PORTRAIT
It is important that the frame (in this case, the flowers) are not totally in focus, otherwise it will be distracting from the face. Therefore it is best to have the flowers as close as possible to the camera lens.

SECRET TRICK

The frame does not need to be in focus. In fact, if it is too sharp it will distract the eye from the subject of the photograph. Use depth of field (see pages 12 and 13 for more information) to make the frame blurred.

1 In the photo above, the focus is on the city skyline. The pier railing is very close to the lens, making it out of focus. The blurry railing serves to emphasize the main subject of the photograph.

2 If the photographer had stepped away from the frame the railing would become more in focus and distracting.

3 Without the frame being included at all, the viewer's eye is not drawn into the photograph in the same way.

Experimenting with
viewpoints

A photograph's viewpoint is determined by the position of the camera. It is decided by where you are placed in comparison with your subject when you take the picture. You can often change a photograph dramatically by experimenting with the viewpoint. Moving the camera up or down, or stepping to one side, for example, can result in a more dramatic image.

MOVE TO THE SIDE AND ZOOM IN

These images show clearly how viewpoint can be used to change a photo, and perhaps make it more interesting.

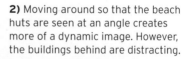

1) This straight-on view shows beach huts with buildings looming behind in the background. The strong point of this photo is its interesting mix of architecture.

2) Moving around so that the beach huts are seen at an angle creates more of a dynamic image. However, the buildings behind are distracting.

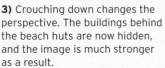

3) Crouching down changes the perspective. The buildings behind the beach huts are now hidden, and the image is much stronger as a result.

These tools will help you experiment with different viewpoints:
• tripod **to hold the camera steady**
• **wide-angle lens to alter the view without you moving**

TAKE PHOTOS FROM ABOVE

Choosing a viewpoint from slightly above has allowed the photographer to include the shadow in the photograph. This has created a more abstract image of the bike.

tripod three-legged device for holding cameras steady
wide-angle lens lens that shows a wide view

SECRET TRICK

Using a **wide-angle lens** will dramatically change the proportions of your subject in the photograph.

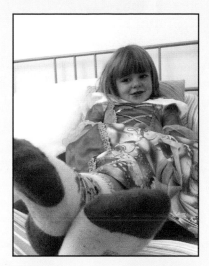

Are the princess's feet really this big? Of course not! A wide-angle lens has been used to make them loom up large at the front of the image.

In the photo above, the iPhone 4 camera is on its widest setting, a digital zoom of 3.9mm. The objects nearest to the lens seem out of proportion.

This kind of lens allows fun compositions, especially when combined with interesting viewpoints and angles.

Capturing
movement

When photographing a moving subject, such as a person walking, a cyclist or a car, you can **freeze the motion by choosing a faster** shutter speed **and taking the photo very quickly. But you should also consider** *when* **to press the shutter.**

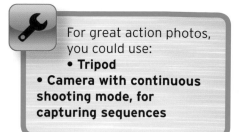

For great action photos, you could use:
- **Tripod**
- **Camera with continuous shooting mode, for capturing sequences**

WHEN TO PRESS THE SHUTTER
Time the moment when you press the shutter so that the subject appears in the correct place. Your action photos will look best with space in front of the subject. That way the subject will appear to be moving into, rather than out of, the photograph. This requires careful composition, and possibly using a tripod to keep your camera steady.

TAKEN AT THE CORRECT MOMENT
The runner is running into the photo frame. This image was taken with a compact camera in sports mode. The camera has automatically used a faster shutter speed to freeze movement.

shutter speed length of time the camera shutter stays open, also called the exposure time

CORRECT MOMENT
The seagull is captured at the right moment in this composition.

WRONG MOMENT
The shutter was pressed too late, the seagull is walking out of the photograph.

SECRET TRICK

With an SLR camera, use some running water to explore the different effects of shutter speeds. Bring a tripod, to guarantee that you don't shake the camera. It is more effective for comparison to keep the composition exactly the same. The slower the shutter speed, the more ghostly the running water will appear.

DIFFERENT USES OF SHUTTER SPEEDS

Do you want to freeze a movement so it looks still, or do you want to capture your subject with an intentional blur, giving it a sense of movement?

At the fast shutter speed of f/4.5, 1/500th of a second, the water droplets are clearly defined.

At f/9, 1/125th of a second, the water droplets are becoming less defined.

At f/18, 1/30th of a second, the water movement appears as one large mass.

At f/22, 1/10th of a second, the water fountain appears to be covered in ice.

These photographs were taken with an SLR camera. In the photo of the boy trapping the ball, the shutter speed has to be 1/500th of a second or faster to freeze the movement of the player. The ball moves even faster, so it might still be blurred. Having a bit of motion blur does add some energy to a sports photograph. In the photo of the boy running, the camera moves with the footballer. This creates a blurred background, but the focus stays on the player.

Notice in these photographs how the change in aperture (the f number) has also affected the depth of field.

Skateboarding
photography

In the mid 1970s, photographer Warren Bolster became head of *Skateboarder* magazine. Bolster was a fearless photographer, regularly putting himself into danger to get unique and beautiful photos. His spectacular images helped to propel skateboarding into the public eye. He inspired the next generation of skateboarders, as well as a whole group of skate photographers.

GETTING INTO SKATEBOARD PHOTOGRAPHY

Skateboard photography is interesting and exciting for a photographer. Many skateboard photographers are skaters themselves. They know which tricks to look for and what to emphasize in their shots. If you're not a skater, maybe you have friends who skateboard? These tips will give your skateboarding images the edge.

TRY A DIFFERENT PERSPECTIVE

Instead of photographing from straight on, try crouching down. Even better, lie on the ground and shoot upward, making the skater look gigantic (you have to be brave to do this!). Also try tilting your camera to add a feeling of dynamic chaos to the photograph.

Photo-editing software can be used to create a skate sequence like this one.

FOCUS ON DETAILS

Don't always photograph the whole skater. Instead, pick out details. For example, you could give attention to the board, crop in on legs and shoes, or include portraits of skaters. Go close up, shoot from a distance, or use a wide-angle lens to include more of the skateboarding environment.

DIFFERENT LIGHTING EFFECTS

Photographing into the light is usually considered a bad idea in photography, but timed correctly, with your skater blocking the light, you will get a **silhouette** effect. On sunny days look for interesting shadows of the skater to include in your shots. Or you could try using your flash during daytime, to give the photo a more hyper-real effect.

silhouette appearing dark but surrounded by light

Look for **diagonals**

In landscapes, many photographs include straight lines such as roads, waterways and fences. Composing your photo so that these run diagonally rather than horizontally is usually seen as more dynamic. It is worth thinking of the balance of a picture in the same way. Generally, an asymmetrical or informal balance is considered more pleasing in a photograph than a symmetrical, formal balance.

ANGLES AND STRAIGHT LINES
America's long, empty roads leading into the vast open landscape provide great photographic subjects. In the colour photo the camera is in the centre of the road, which disappears into the middle of the photo. In the black-and-white photo, a diagonal effect has been achieved by moving to the side of the road, which then appears at an angle.

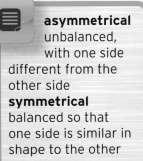

asymmetrical unbalanced, with one side different from the other side
symmetrical balanced so that one side is similar in shape to the other

PHOTO BALANCE

'Balance' is a way of describing where the main subject of a photo appears, and where other objects appear in relation to it. Try placing the main subject off-centre, then balancing it with other smaller or noticeable objects. Your photo will work better than if you placed the subject in the centre. Here are some examples.

In the first of the two photos above, with the main subject right in the centre of the photograph, the photo has a pleasing balance. However, when it is placed off-centre the image becomes stronger.

In the photo on the right, the beach chairs are the main subject, and are off-centre and diagonal. The small trolley on the right balances out the photograph.

SECRET TRICK

The 'rule of thirds' is a principle taught in graphic design and photography. It is based on the theory that the viewer's eyes naturally go to a point about two-thirds up the page.

1 Try composing a photograph so that it visually divides into thirds, horizontally or vertically. You should find that you achieve a pleasing informal or asymmetrical balance in your photograph.

2 In the photograph above, the rule of thirds works horizontally and vertically. Horizontally, the low sign appears in the lower third *and* the left-hand third. Vertically, the tall sign is in the upper third *and* the right-hand third.

Taking
portraits

Lighting and composition
are the main factors that will
produce a great portrait. You
might like to bring out the
details of a face with hard
lighting, **or depict a young
child's face with** soft lighting. **In
this section you will learn how
to use lighting to create perfect
portraits in a variety of styles.**

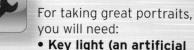

For taking great portraits,
you will need:
• **Key light (an artificial
light, sunlight or daylight
through a window)**
• **Reflector (light-reflective
material for bouncing light
back at the subject)**

Subject
Light
Camera

THE 45° LIGHT
This style of portrait revolves
around one **key light**, set
at 45° to the subject's face
and slightly higher. Another,
less-bright light can then be
used to lighten the shadows,
softening the contrast. Here
a reflector has been used to
bounce light under and into
the eyes, and a hair light has
been used to make the hair
shine.

BROAD-PORTRAIT LIGHTING
The face of the sitter is turned
away from the key light (in
this case, a window lighting
the side of the girl's face). In
the second photo, a reflector
has been used to bounce
light into the darker side of
the girl's face. This softens
the lighting and produces a
nice reflection in both eyes,
bringing them to life.

SHORT-PORTRAIT LIGHTING
Here the face is turned
towards the key light, so the
'short' side of the girl's face
is lit. In the second image, a
reflector has been used to
light up the darker side of the
face and add life to the eyes.

SECRET TRICK

To shoot portraits on a compact camera, use portrait mode. This makes the camera choose a larger aperture, giving your photograph less depth of field. The focus will be on the face, not the surroundings.

To create a more flattering look, take the picture with your zoom lens fully extended (if it's fully in it will distort the face). Also make sure that light is reflected in the sitter's eyes. If you don't have a reflector, a white sheet will do the same job!

Here the camera angle creates a powerful image of the girl.

SPLIT-PORTRAIT LIGHTING
The key light is so far off to the side that only one half of the face is lit.

hard light direct key light, with no softening
key light dominant lighting in a photograph
soft light indirect, soft key light

REMBRANDT-PORTRAIT LIGHTING
This is the name given to a lighting effect that the famous painter Rembrandt often used. It is a form of short-portrait lighting, with the shadow from the nose connecting with the shadow on the side of the face. This creates a triangle of light on the side of the face.

BUTTERFLY-PORTRAIT LIGHTING
Butterfly-portrait lighting is achieved by having direct light high above the subject, casting a downward shadow. It is named after the shape of the shadow created directly beneath the nose.

Self-portrait
photography

Taking self-portraits is a good way to practice how to light, compose and expose a portrait shot. Self-portraits can be close-ups or wider shots showing you and your surroundings. (If you want to show more of your environment, use the camera's self-timer button.)

These self-portraits are by Vanessa Jones, and were inspired by the work of Cindy Sherman.

BASIC SELF-PORTRAITS

Simply holding the camera just a little above you and looking up before pressing the shutter will produce quite a good self-portrait. If you'd like to achieve something more special, though, follow these guidelines to create stunning photos of yourself.

SIMPLE TECHNIQUES

Paying attention to your key light source will improve your photograph. Light from a 45° angle and slightly higher will give an interesting light on your face. Or you could try direct light from above. This always comes out well, especially when you look straight up into the camera. (See pages 28 and 29 for more lighting ideas.)

USING MIRRORS

Using mirrors can be a very effective way of taking self-portraits. Compose your photo so that you include the real you and some of your reflection, or vice versa. This might require a tripod, to steady your digital compact or SLR camera. Focusing on yourself can be complicated, therefore if you have the choice with your camera, set a smaller aperture, to get a greater depth of field (see pages 12 and 13 for more information).

Self-portraiture allows you to be creative, so have fun with it. These photos were taken on an iPhone camera with the Hipstomatic app.

BACKDROPS

Take care in choosing the right backdrop. If it is cluttered behind your head in a way that will spoil the photograph, clear the space. If that is not possible, change the camera angle.

Taking **landscapes**

You do not have to be in the countryside to take landscape photographs. Right outside your front door there might be a street scene to photograph. A nearby park may give you a chance to try different depths of field in a non-urban setting. If you live by the sea, practice composition on the beach and the big skies, or the promenade.

For landscape photography:
- **Tripod**
- **Wide-angle lens (with an SLR camera)**

Want to find out more about taking great landscape shots? Head to: **www.acblack.com/ instantexpert**

KEY FACTORS IN LANDSCAPE PHOTOGRAPHY

The factors to concentrate on in landscape shots are composition and light. If your camera allows, using different lenses and apertures to control the depth of field will give you more control over how your photograph looks.

LANDSCAPES WITH A CAMERA PHONE

Look for interesting light and skies, and compose your photo carefully. Using composition techniques such as framing, diagonals and the rule of thirds will make your picture stronger. In the example above, railings along a seafront promenade create a frame leading into the picture.

LANDSCAPES WITH A COMPACT CAMERA

Follow the same composition guidelines as above, but set your camera to landscape mode. The camera will then choose a small aperture, creating a great depth of field. Also, when you are composing the photo you will usually find it better to have your zoom lens at its shortest setting, as this allows a bigger view.

The longer focal length of the upper photograph (taken at f/8 with a 45mm lens) gives a narrower view. The shorter, wide-angle focal length of the lower image (taken at f/8 with a 24mm lens) shows more landscape.

LANDSCAPES WITH AN SLR CAMERA

The SLR camera has the same functions as a compact camera if you set it to automatic or landscape mode. Or you can change to a wide-angle lens, which allows a wider perspective. With the camera in aperture priority setting (Av), you can use the aperture controls to affect depth of field.

ISO scale of a camera sensor's sensitivity; high ISO numbers result in more sensitivity and increase the camera's ability to take pictures in low light

SECRET TRICK

Compact and SLR cameras allow you to alter your film sensor sensitivity, or **ISO**, setting.

1 In darker light conditions, increase your ISO setting from the normal 100 ASA to anything up to 3200 ASA. This allows a smaller aperture setting, increasing depth of field and putting more of the photo in focus.

2 On an SLR camera, choosing a faster shutter speed to match your higher ISO setting will make it possible to hand hold your camera in low-light conditions.

The landscape changes dramatically at night. What appears normal during the day can become beautiful when painted with lights.

3 Remember that anything over 800 ASA will increase the 'camera noise', or graininess, of your photographs.

Still-life photography

For shooting great still lifes, you may need:
- **Tripod**
- Macro **lens or setting**

Still-life is one of the most creative types of photography. You have complete control over the subject matter, composition, and lighting. So next time you feel like there is nothing to photograph – go and shoot a fantastic image of some vegetables you find in your fridge!

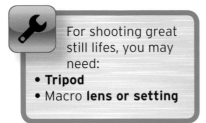

A base of crunched-up tissue paper adds extra texture to this still life.

The cool glass background suits this game-tech stuff and creates interesting reflections.

1) CONSIDER COMPOSITION
Choose the object or objects to photograph. Experiment with different groups of objects, and arrange and re-arrange them several times to get a composition that effectively gets across the message of the photo. In the photos above, moving the lipstick has made it less the main object. It is more about the grouping of the subjects. The light reflects more evenly on the lipstick too.

2) CHOOSE THE BACKGROUND
The background should reinforce the photo's message, without distracting from the main subjects. Picking between light, dark, cloth, paper, velvet, reflective surfaces or mirrors is an important choice. Sometimes a busy background suits the chosen subject.

SECRET TRICK

Create a still life by photographing everyday, motionless scenes. Even the breakfast table with empty cereal bowls and half-drunk cups of tea, if composed right, can make a great still life.

Even things you would normally think of as dull can be used as interesting backgrounds. In the photograph on the left, a steamed-up window has been used to create a setting for an assortment of funny figures.

macro lens or setting that magnifies the subject, making it as big or bigger than in real life

3) LIGHTING

Most still-life photographers use natural light as much as possible, because natural light gives a special glow and effect to the composition. They place the subjects near a window or a light source. A simple desk lamp is a good alternative light source. Use white cards as reflectors, bouncing light into the shadowy areas.

Want to know more about different ways to light your photographs? Go to: **www.acblack.com/ instantexpert**

Still life set up without a reflector to light up darker areas of the photograph.

This is the same image taken using a white-card reflector. See how the rose on the right is lit evenly.

This is the final still life arrangement, with the colour altered slightly using photo-editing software.

Street photography

Street photography looks at city life through the people who live it. The street photographer documents human activity, always looking to capture a special moment. Over-familiarity with our environment can make it difficult to see that special moment or subject. As a street photographer you have to be confident, get up close, follow your instincts for a good photo, and detect the moment to take the best image.

Taken with an SLR camera.

ALWAYS CARRY A CAMERA

Always have a camera with you. This means you are always ready to capture the shot. Today's camera phones make it easy to have a camera with you wherever you go.

Taken with an iPhone 4.

FYI!

Set your camera to automatic mode, so that you can concentrate on capturing the decisive moment.

PICK YOUR PLACE AND TIME

For street photography, it is a good idea to decide on a particular area or street before you set off. Also choose a time or day of the week that will be busy. If you are feeling intimidated about taking out your camera, start at a market scene, a street fair or a sports event. People will be distracted and pay less attention to you taking pictures.

Compact cameras are great for street photography. All these images were taken using a compact camera.

TAKE MULTIPLE PHOTOS

If a scene particularly grabs your interest, take more than one image. Watch a bit longer, see the scene develop and change. This will allow you to pick out the best moments for your photo.

TRY ODD ANGLES

You don't always have to photograph people from in front or looking at the camera. If you like the scene and the main subjects are looking away, it is still worth a picture. Sometimes getting a shot without the face, for example from behind, can add a bit of mystery to the photo too.

Colour or black and white?

Colour photography is more popular than black and white. Black and white or monochrome **photography relies more on composition, form and lighting. It used to be seen as a more artistic form of photography. However, in the 1970s the famous American art photographer William Eggleston changed this perception, by working entirely in colour.**

LANDSCAPES

Whether to photograph landscapes in colour or black and white might depend on the time of year, the place and the time of day. For example, an autumn beech-tree forest in colour will show the change of the season, and tell a story in a way that black and white could not. But black and white draws attention to form and shapes in a way that colour cannot - especially if the light causes shadows to fall.

The same subject can have different messages, depending on whether you use black and white or colour. Photographing the burned Joshua trees in black and white enhances their fire-damaged texture. In colour, the yellow of the earth emphasizes the heat and dryness of the Californian desert.

At night, colour works really well. The black background enhances the illuminated colours in the image.

If you are not sure whether to use colour or black and white, take your photos in colour.

1 After you have imported photos into your computer, use photo-editing software to create a black-and-white image. Usually you have to 'desaturate 100%' to achieve this.

PEOPLE

When photographing people, consider the message of your portrait and whether there are colours in the picture that you would like to bring out. For the cobbler and his wife, who follow a traditional trade, the choice of black and white fits the subject well. In the 1940s-style portrait, the red lipstick and powdery pink of the feather boa give the photograph the feel of the correct historical period.

STILL LIFES

As with portraits, try to match your choice to the subject and message of the photograph. Black and white can create a sense of timelessness or history. Colour adds texture and tone to a still-life subject. In the photo above centre, the blue glass bottle becomes the main focus point in a way it does not in black and white. The warm natural light picks out the texture and colour of the wall.

Compare the black-and-white image to the colour one on the left. In black and white, the bottles on the shelves become less important. You notice how the light falls and the texture of the glass instead.

2 Next, lighten or darken and increase your contrast to achieve a monochrome version of your picture. This way, you will have both colour and black-and-white versions available.

monochrome
one colour

Digital resolutions
explained

Digital cameras today are much less expensive and better than ever before. They offer a wide range of quality. The first thing most people look at when choosing a camera is the number of megapixels (MP) it can record. The higher the number of megapixels, the more detail the camera will be able to capture in a photograph. If you print out the photograph, it should be clearer, sharper and brighter.

This image does not contain many pixels. **Printed tiny it looks fine, but as the image is printed bigger it becomes more and more grainy.**

CAMERA PHONES
Camera phones usually take every photo with a set amount of MP. You cannot adjust them to take low, medium, or high-quality images. Normally camera phones have between 1MP and 5MP.

COMPACT CAMERAS
When buying a compact camera look out for a high MP. You can then adjust the camera to take high-quality images for bigger prints, or low-resolution images for snap shots or uploading to the Internet. Unless you are planning large prints, it is usually best to keep the camera on a medium setting so that you don't run out of **memory card** space.

dpi short for 'dots per inch', a measure of how clearly something is printed
memory card card in a camera, which stores photos
pixelated grainy and with blocky edges
pixels tiny dots that make up a digital image

SECRET TRICK

High megapixel cameras record a lot of detail and use up the memory quickly. Buy a large capacity or additional memory cards to save the disappointment of running out of space.

Memory cards come in various formats so check which type your camera uses before you buy.

This is a very pixelated, **low image-quality print. There is no visible detail in the dog's coat.**

FYI!

The camera with the highest megapixels (570MP!) is an astronomy camera worth $35 000 000.

This much clearer image has higher image quality. There is fine detail and no pixelation.

YOUR DIGITAL SLR CAMERA

Digital SLR cameras usually come with a high amount of megapixels. In the image-quality setting of your camera you can choose the quality. Small, medium or large image output is sometimes also separated as fine or standard quality. Professional cameras additionally come with a RAW setting, which records even more information, but can only be printed after editing in Photoshop or similar photo-editing software.

HOW BIG CAN I PRINT?

For better prints change your image '**dpi**' to 300dpi. For uploading images to websites or for email, set it to 72dpi.

If you want to print...	Take a look at...
Pocket-sized snaps for sharing with friends	Any camera with 3MP or more will produce great results on a print up to 15cm x 10cm (6" x 4")
Larger prints to put in an album	A camera around 5MP will give you great pictures on a print up to 20cm x 15cm (8" x 6")
Pictures for framing and hanging	A camera with between 5MP and 8MP can produce quality prints up to 25cm x 20cm (10" x 8")
Large photos or posters	10MP cameras will give you prints up to A4 size, and 20MP or more will print at up to A3 size

Troubleshooting

If your photos aren't turning out right, there's usually a fairly simple explanation. Although modern cameras can seem quite complicated, especially SLRs, the technical basics of photography are actually simple. Is the lens focusing properly? Is it letting in the right amount of light for the photograph to be clear and well lit? If so, your photographs should turn out well. If they do not, this troubleshooting guide should help you put things right.

PROBLEM 1: CAMERA SHAKE AND BLURRED PHOTOS

There is nothing more annoying than taking what you think are great photographs, then realizing when you look at them on the computer that they are out of focus. This is often caused by your hands shaking the camera during a long exposure time or shutter speed. You could:
• Use a tripod to steady your camera.
• Open the aperture, which will make the shutter speed faster.
• Increase the ISO from the normal 100ASA to anything up to 1600ASA, which will cause the camera to select a faster shutter speed.

PROBLEM 2: DARK IMAGES

Your photos will come out too dark (or 'underexposed') if there is not enough light or you have chosen the wrong aperture/shutter speed combination.
• Not enough light can be fixed by raising the ISO setting. You might also want to use a flash.
• If you have chosen an aperture such as f/22 to achieve great depth of field but there is not enough light for it then the camera will not cope. Open the aperture to let more light through the lens.
• When you first compose the photo and half-press the shutter button, try to make sure the camera does its exposure reading on the main subject you are photographing.

PROBLEM 3: WASHED-OUT, TOO-BRIGHT IMAGES

Your photos will come out too light (or 'overexposed') if there is too much light around and the camera is set on an open aperture (for example f/4) and cannot choose a fast enough shutter speed. Every camera has a limit to the highest possible shutter speeds it can manage.
• Make sure the camera is on the lowest ISO setting.
• Reduce the aperture setting by choosing a higher f-stop number, e.g. f/16.
• In bright sunlight, SLR users can use a filter on their lens to block out some light.

PROBLEM 4: PIXELATED PRINTS

If your prints come out pixelated (grainy and with blocky edges), it is usually because the camera was not set to a high enough resolution, or because the printing process has not been properly set up.
• Set your camera to the highest picture resolution when taking the photos.
• After you have imported them into your computer, change the dpi from 72 to 300dpi at the 'wanted printing' size.

• Set your printer to match the paper quality that you are printing on.

PROBLEM 5: TOO MUCH CONTRAST

In some extreme-light situations, the camera's image sensor is not able to pick up the whole range of light and expose an image correctly. In this case:
• Either select the part of the scene that is most important to expose correctly, or;
• Choose a subject in between the darkest and lightest elements of the picture to take the light reading.

PROBLEM 6: IMAGES OUT OF FOCUS OR CAMERA CAN'T FOCUS

If you are using the autofocus setting but haven't composed and locked the focus on your main subject by pressing the shutter button halfway before you take the picture, your image is likely to be blurred.
• Always make sure you focus on your main subject, press the shutter button halfway, then recompose if necessary and press the shutter button all the way.
• In darker light situations, SLR cameras might find it difficult to find the focus point. If this happens, change your focus to the manual focus setting, and use the focus ring on the lens instead.

PROBLEM 7: LENS FLARE

If your photographs suffer from **lens flare**:
• Be careful not to photograph into the light.
• SLR users can add a lens cap to the end of their lens to cut down on lens flare.
• Decrease the aperture.

lens flare unplanned blocks of light in photographs

Technical photography
language

aperture mechanism inside the lens controlling amount of light coming in

asymmetrical unbalanced, with one side different from the other side

camera obscura lightproof box with a small hole that lets through enough light to make an upsidedown image

depth of field distance between the nearest and farthest objects that are in sharp focus

dpi short for 'dots per inch', a measure of how clearly something is printed

exposure how much light a camera lens lets in

hard light direct key light, with no softening

high key mostly light, including whites

ISO scale of a camera sensor's sensitivity; high ISO numbers result in more sensitivity and increase the camera's ability to take pictures in low light

key light dominant lighting in a photograph

lens flare unplanned blocks of light in photographs

low key mostly dark, including black

macro lens or setting that magnifies the subject, making it as big or bigger than in real life

memory card card in a camera, which stores photos

monochrome one colour

pixels tiny dots that make up a digital image

pixelated grainy and with blocky edges

shutter button trigger for the shutter mechanism of the camera

shutter speed length of time the camera shutter stays open, also called the exposure time

silhouette appearing dark but surrounded by light

SLR short for Single Lens Reflex

soft light indirect, softer key light

symmetrical balanced so that one side is a similar shape to the other

tripod three-legged device for holding cameras steady

wide-angle lens lens that shows a wide view

zoom lengthen or shorten the lens, so that the subject seems closer or further away

Further information

BOOKS

These books will all help you develop your photography skills. They are written for adults, but are clear and simple enough for younger readers to use.

The Photographer's Eye: Composition and Design for Better Digital Photos Michael Freeman (ILEX Publishers, 2007) This book will help you to develop a photographer's eye for a good image, capturing the right moment and developing your own style.

Understanding Exposure: How to Shoot Great Photographs with Any Camera Bryan Peterson (Amphoto Books, 3rd edition, 2010) This book will make you more explorative in your photography and help you to move away from relying on the camera's automatic settings.

The Complete Guide to Digital Black & White Photography Michael Freeman (Lark Publishers, 2010) This is an excellent guide if you want to learn more about black and white photography.

WEBSITES

www.explainthatstuff.com/ photography/ A general site that is useful for all kinds of information about photography.

www.facethelight.com/aperture.php This site explains aperture and its effect on your photographs in detail.

www.tutorial9.net/tutorials/ photography-tutorials/troubleshooting/ Excellent for further troubleshooting information if pages 42 and 43 have not been able to help you solve your photography problems.

Photography timeline

1826

Nicéphore Niépce takes the first permanent photograph, using a camera obscura to burn an image of his estate in France. He names his technique 'heliography', meaning 'sun drawing'. The exposure takes eight hours and fades considerably, but an image is still visible on the plate today.

1839

Louis Daguerre patents the 'daguerreotype'. He photographs a Paris street scene from his apartment window. The long exposure of several minutes means moving objects like pedestrians and carriages don't appear in the photo. An unidentified man who stops for a shoeshine does remain still enough to become the first person ever photographed.

1839

William Fox Talbot invents the positive/negative process. His 'talbotype' process is the first to use a negative from which many positive prints can be made.

1861

The first colour photograph is shown by James Clerk Maxwell. The Scottish scientist creates a colour image by combining three black-and-white images that had been passed through red, green and blue filters into a single image.

1871

Gelatine emulsion is invented by the English photographer and physician Richard Maddox. Photographers were then able to use glass negative plates with a dried gelatin emulsion on them. These could be stored, so photographers no longer needed portable darkrooms to develop their photographs.

William Fox Talbot, one of the early pioneers of photography.

1878

English photographer Eadweard Muybridge captures high-speed movement. He uses the new emulsion to record the photo sequence of a galloping horse. The shutter is triggered by the horse running past 12 cameras, each fitted with a trip wire.

1900

George Eastman of Kodak invents film with a base that is flexible, unbreakable, and can be rolled. First mass-produced box camera appears, the 'Brownie' by Kodak.

1907

The first colour photography process, 'Autochrome Lumiere', is marketed by the Lumiere brothers in France.

1923

Doctor Harold Edgerson invents Xenon flash and strobe photography.

1925
Leica introduces the 35mm camera, designed by Oskar Barnack.

1936
First film-based single lens reflex camera (SLR) is produced.

1948
Polaroid produces the first instant-image camera. As soon as the photograph is taken, it begins developing into a print, which can be viewed soon afterwards.

1959
AGFA introduces the first fully automatic camera.

1961
The concept of digitizing images is put forward by Eugene F. Lally.

1968
The Earth is photographed from the Moon.

1975
Stephen Sasson invents the digital camera for Kodak. The camera weighs 3.6kg/8lb and records black-and-white images on a cassette tape.

1981
Sony produce the first consumer camera, the Mavica Electronic, which does not require film. Images are recorded onto a mini disc and then played on a video reader connected to a monitor.

1986
Kodak scientists invent the first megapixel sensor, which can record 1.4 megapixels and produce a clear, snapshot-sized print.

1988 Fuji release the DS-1P camera, which can store digital images.

1991
Kodak releases the first professional digital SLR camera. At 1.3 megapixels with a Nikon F-3 body it was aimed at photojournalists.

1994
Digital compact cameras, the Apple Quick Take 100 and the Kodak DC40, become available for the consumer market.

2000
The first camera phone is marketed by Sharp. The Sharp JSH04 had a 0.1 megapixels sensor.

2001
Canon releases their EOS 1D camera, with up to 6.3 megapixels.

2004
Kodak announces that it will not produce any more film cameras.

2006
Nikon and Canon stop film-camera production.

2010
Sony Ericsson develops the highest megapixel camera phone so far. The S006 has a 16-megapixel sensor.

This camera was made by Zeiss, a famous camera company and lens manufacturer.

Index